Stars in the Junkyard

by Sharon Berg

Cover photograph 'Beetle and the Big Dipper' by Tomas Lollike. https://photo.lollike.dk

Author photograph by Tom Gannon Hamilton.

Sharon Berg, 1954

Stars in the Junkyard

Poetry

ISBN: 978-93-90202-23-2

Published by Cyberwit
HIG 45, KAUSHAMBI KUNJ, KALINDIPURAM,
ALLAHABAD - 211011 (U.P.) INDIA +(91) 9415091004
www.cyberwit.net/

Dedication

*For my daughters, Ila and Brynna (Kirsten),
who are both working their way through
and out of the labyrinth.*

5

Table of Contents

Honesty is more than not lying. It is truth telling, truth speaking, truth living, and truth loving.

— *James E. Faust*

1

Drawing Maps

Stars in the Junkyard

A child let loose from the house
you stood on the back stoop
gazing at stars like pinhole lights
in a sapphire flannel blanket.
Crickets in moonlit fields rubbed the hairs
of rough legs along fiddled bodies
singing, *I am here, let me in,*
as if they could be refused.
Cricket on the hearth brings company,
the old wives' tale.
You and I know miles of corduroy fields
are bridged with memory
where the corn stands tall
and night is the flannel in your mouth,
shoved there for silence.

In the house, the adults were loud.
Dishes clanging tunes in the galvanized tub,
your errand a bucket of water
cold as metal from the outdoor pump.
That pump was always a green cricket
calling out for love
in starlight away from the house.
I am here, let me out.
No one to hear the progression of that tune,
you sang until it wore a groove in the brain.

1953. 1954. You and I were raised
with a view on the same backyard,
between that house and the other
— converted animal housing,

a pig barn or chicken coop,
the neighbours poorer than us —
lay the wrecks of used bodies,
the cars our fathers had abandoned.

The shouts coming across
were like the children in that yard
— dirty, half-meant —
their door propped for a cross-breeze.
Between their shouts, like bells,
the tinkling of laughter.
Laughter in the house behind
you standing at the pump,
arm aching, pump water spilling.
You drank those musical notes
wondering how anyone could laugh
with a throat so parched for love.

But starlight gathered like silver
across those wasted bodies in the yard
— our fathers' dreams —
a harem of submissive curves
in midnight blue or a red as dangerous
as putting it all into a woman they wanted
on the tarmac, foot to the floor.
Those cars were easy engines purring
beneath an indigo flannel
of what might have been, the keys
to everything that moved from our yard
in the greasy pockets of our fathers' greens.

You cherished the stars
collecting on glass and chrome in the junkyard.
In sunlight, the stars waited close,

as heat baked into those hoods,
a secret galaxy spinning white and celestial
as your first trip out of the body
under his hairy moons.
I am here, let me out.
And he did not stop tending to simple functions,
the cylinders and pistons,
looting from one body to complete another,
his hands like love in the dark oil.
Those hands that carried food to the table
with a ceremony something like love.

One day he took an empty oil can and shears.
As you stood watching,
the smell of dirty engines smarting your nose
like his scent,
he cut the rough shape of a star
and wiped it on his sleeve.
The cut edge of each arm dangerous and curled,
he pinned it over your heart.
All these years of wishing on stars,
only now you realize
this was the star that set you free.

We have both stepped in and out of our bodies
with our arms crooked for love.
Children dragged up by the scruff of our fears,
wearing hand prints on our faces
— five-fingered stars —
we worried two questions throughout our lives.
Why me? and *Why not me?*
You and I — if any two people —
should slip into each other like starlight
arriving.

Everyone has pathetic stories.
For us the stories are amplified in the children
we could not carry out of confusion in those houses
— your children rocked to sleep by your ex-wife,
the first of mine, a promise kept
in someone else's marriage —
We've been singing these tunes so long.
Now you reach past the echo for a refrain,
standing by the door as if distance
could unmake what is here.
Like the man sang in that famous tune —
The greatest thing you'll ever learn
is just to love
and be loved in return.

Genesis

The stars are shifting on their axis,
each one a constant friend
through the pitching nightmare
of these transitional years.

Even the calendar
is untrue these days,
never presenting the moon
in its old dependable way.

Overhead, the constellations dance,
my perspective altered
like a ripple in glass.
A foggy figure presents on the horizon.

You and I know nothing of its making,
only note that each constellation
swings over to allow room,
each star song slips into a new key.

In 100 years we may decipher those tunes.
For now we can only collect data
on the orbit of friends, the quality of life
persuaded from water and dust.

I write notes here, a diary of changes.
Stubborn seeds germinate in the barest earth.
I study the pithy sky. The stars are old friends —
just now one swallowed its tail and blinked out.

Every living thing
challenges its finite seasons.
Neither the process nor *The Book of Telling*
will be finished in our time.

One clear note echoes
across space between us
and, in its echo,
shifts to become another.

Difficult

I am difficult,
You are right in that, brother.
I am as difficult as you are to love
with your shifting moods
and world-blaming pains.
I am the family truth-teller
no matter your idea of private.
That makes me painful
for anyone in my family
or closely associated
to love.

Listen, I do not write
to deliver beautifications
for the sake of family or lovers.
I do not write to assuage
your conscience or mine
by blaming others.
I write to understand
truth in the development
of human relations.
I speak to my own
experience.

Allow me my voice.

Shucking Corn

You hold a paper bag between your knees,
its neck turned down like a handmade toque.
You hold the naked cob in both hands,
removing its whisper of green cloth.
It's translucent as anything that doesn't see light.
You've been instructed how to do this,
every hair catching at the back of the throat,
a cough that won't leave.
You sit outside the house,
your lip line red and unpretending.
How you resent this thing you do for the family,
shucking corn for their table
and your daily bread.
You sit on a pretty slab patio
on a quiet street in an ordinary subdivision.
You would hate this chore as much
in the middle of a field where the corn
stands tall as a man.
You know there isn't a child
anywhere, anytime,
who has chosen to shuck corn.

Hansel and Gretel

Siblings lost in the forest,
we meet at its horrible center
though we come by different routes,
set loose with the crumbs in our pockets
and glad for simple company.
The adults of that house in the clearing
smiled sweetly and kissed our foreheads,
cried and took our hands to their breast.
This is my heart, my mother said.
See how it beats for you?
It beats, and beats, and beats —
but when I am happy it slows.
She smiled, but the language of our home
was fear. Jealousy was a brute
kicking the heart into double-time.
Double-tongued, the hearts in our home
drummed codes for everything
that could not be said.
He loves her, he loves me not.
She loves him, she loves me not.
They love each other, they love us not.
Until we dared to enter the forest
(green-scaled beast, dragon hunched over
secrets and breathing fire at sunset)
we could not have known
we would find each other
by entering the dragon's belly.

The Door On Privacy

We are sitting with our coffees,
my brother and I, talking
when floorboards outside the room cry
          someone curious is listening
          on the other side of the wood
in this all-male house my female voice
attracts an eavesdropper

We pause, you in mid-sentence
me half-giggling to think
          that any one could
          be so nosy —
but it isn't funny anymore
as the handle rotates
          the locked door is tried
          that someone become a nervy
'who's there?' that doesn't answer
slipping down the hall
          followed by grumbles of the floor

Servitude

my mother's mother, born in the 1800s
the first of thirteen children
dirt poor and surrounded by Irish famine
sold when she was eight years old
becoming indentured to
a Canadian farmer
near Belleville, Ontario

maid, cook, cleaner, and field hand
she *dressed* children older than she was
fed the animals
helped to bring in the harvest
bound to do nothing else
'til she turned twenty-one

didn't eat the same as she cooked
for the family she served,
a blanket on the kitchen floor her bed
stunted to 5 foot 2 inches
lucky to receive her freedom
before the work she did killed her

long before my grandmother's plight
King James I of England's proclamation
meant debtors in Ireland, thieves and traitors
were shipped to the West Indies, Barbados,
Virginia, New England and Australia
some children as young as 8 years

indentured servants to the wealthy
families ripped apart when the poor

found no alternative for survival
selling their children's services
as indentured slaves
whatever name you give them

my grandmother was a slave
who never returned to Ireland
losing touch with her birth family
growing into a bitter woman
who manipulated
family connections

I hold no grudges
loving her for surviving
and her few tender
moments

Statues

I wait by my father's shoulder
in the workshop as he fiddles with three
coloured wires, replaces corroded washers
in a gritty engine, so intent
on putting machinery back-to-right
he doesn't realize I am waiting
for something simple.

Squatting on the stained floor
nuts and bolts scattered in sawdust,
he tells me how the wires are coded:
red positive, black or blue negative.
Silently, we make that toolbox
our contract of love,
the act of handing him the right wrench
demonstrates my belief in his ability
to make a thing right
if only he puts his hands on it.

But I learned early, the limit of my ability
to play statue was the pins and needles
in a game of wait
misinterpreted.

Willow

for my father, born on the frontier in 1916

all things begin in dust
or the memory of dust
with hands
or the absence of hands
in silence
and in telling

my father
remembers the endless prairie
on the night his mother died
through the absence
of hands

she had five healthy children
and a new baby
she had an abscessed tooth
and retained placenta
a richer family
and a husband blinded by pride

my father's father shut out
charity from the town folk
refusing assistance from the dentist
not allowing the midwife
to assist his wife
she died in agony

today the judgment would be
death through negligence

my grandmother was 32

the rough hand of justice
might have fallen
yet family and villagers
brewed their resentments in silence

at 12, my father
was apprenticed to manhood
his father's hands laid over his
on the carpenter's plane and auger
he learned the beauty
of hands turned to a task
and doing it well
already knowing the brutality
of hands withheld

and dust blew
through the rough log house
dust of the prairie
settling over his mother's bones
meeting dust of the yellow sky
as the money for building
dried up
on the dust bowl prairie of '29
villagers bolting their doors
my grandfather becoming
an apparition, revenant
with a Bible spread across his knees

necessity became
the mother of contrivance
father and son building incubators
in abandoned grain elevators

on the edge of town
new chicken farmers
the incubators cooked
they lost 500 chicks

my aunt replaced her mother
in the kitchen, her hands
blistered by chores
she grew vegetables in the dust
decades later, her brothers report
She made meals from nothing
but my father still refuses lamb
50 years on, mutton his grandparents sent
to feed their lost daughter's children
still gristly in his mind

at Christmas or Thanksgiving
these siblings gather
for feasts with their children
to share their versions
of childhood well-remembered
not from them would we hear
of their mother's passing
or childhood's empty belly
or the whispering behind hands
in that tiny village
on the dust bowl prairie

instead my grandmother Celia's sisters
cornered my mother
Did your husband ever say
what his father had done?
my mother dumbfounded
unable to keep them silent

in her child's hearing
God punishes in God's way
they said

suddenly I understood my grandfather
locked in silence, the Bible on his lap
resisting grandchildren on his knee
his eyes always fixed on the distance
his hands full of Parkinson's shake
forever signing silent crosses
against evil whispers

my father told us only
of long, hot summers fencing
on his uncle's sheep farm
how they split a fallen willow
to pound the posts into hard prairie
the next spring so wet
most of the posts sprouted
leaves adorning the fence line

years later
the thickened trunks of willow grown
around nail and wire, it surprises me only
how deeply we depend upon
this image of green life
wrapping around nails in the post
all of our children taking leaf
no matter how we split the old tree
no matter what poor dust
they must root in

Coming of Age

for Joan, Pam and Sara

I know what I would be
if I hadn't any babies. The usual pattern:
runaway, selling my ass
for another snort, slow suicide.
These women nod, seeing that progression
daily, in their clients. I can still taste
the bitter stuff in my nose, remember
the constant sniffle, body
shaking with impatience for the bars to open
or another noseful.
Dry Ontario Sundays —
a nightmare of fitful sleep
or running around to every friend's house
for a beer. Getting pregnant that time
stopped me cold.
Slipping into a warm bath now,
I face the scalloped mirror hung low
on a wall the colour of vulvas, examining
my body, four months out of its fourth pregnancy.
Memory is a physical response,
the baby's head still crowning.

At 16, my body waited
under its screen of clothes
— getting wet at mention of cock
and tits, drying up with talk of love.
And I was lucky, my first lover
waiting three months in the same bed,
undressing me over and over

for the canvas. He taught me to see
my body as a masterpiece, Naples yellow
highlighting umber with rosy
madder shadows. Three years later,
he called me his crazy nympho, almost
banking on it when the coke was hard to get.
Another month would have done it,
maybe less. We were both
that close for the sake of snorting.

And that word *love* still disturbs me.
Love was always five times my size,
five times my age —
pulled out by its roots
and shoved back, wrongly.
I plotted my escape, but Law brings back
runaways... until at sixteen, blind justice
switches sides unknowing, the self
a prisoner of its adolescent body.
I escaped by inches.

I moved out: that was one inch.
I took a lover unlike my father:
that was two inches.
He didn't beat me, let me grow some:
those were inches three and four.
Years later, pregnant with our third child,
I hadn't moved another inch
until I decided to keep the baby
and leave her father.
Suddenly I moved ahead in feet
not inches, and still I was only standing
outside my parents' bedroom door.
Every lover has helped to release

the woman inside me.
Remarkable, as they all carved
cruel tattoos on my skin.

Inch by inch, I banish hairy shadows,
every closet revealing family bones.
One shadow builds on another, the face
over breakfast the same, yet unlike
the nightmare skeleton that wore his desires.
The roles in our home reversed, child
giving the parent comfort.
For years afterward, the obscenity of misused power
(a child tricked into adult roles by fairy tales
and magic shows) meant there was no trusting
childhood games on anyone's knees,
or bedtime stories without an edge, or toothpaste
kisses before bed, or liking oneself
in any role.

At 13, hissing voices told social workers,
"It wasn't me. Someone else, maybe.
But she enticed, let her brother fondle."
They told their story over and over,
until even their lies
made better sense. And still,
there was no stopping it.
Social workers sent the child to a psychiatrist.
"Why do you hurt them
with these stories?" he asked.
My cries should have deafened but
the walls soaked them up
as my mother led my pubescent brother
to her revenging bed — enough said.

Double wrong. My parents set up wars of affection
over the dinner table. Whatever he had done
she would top with a demonstration
before us all. If I complained
I lost my supper.
The family had already lost
its comprehension of normal.
How I finally made flight,
I barely know.
Out at 16, inches out.
But no closets could contain them.

At 21, alone and pregnant,
clean, but the taste of coke still rusting my nose,
I opened doors, seeking even those
rough silhouettes of familial belonging.
Now, I am eight years more sure.
They corrupt all they touch with caresses
and believe themselves ordinary.
My younger brother, still there,
would rock my daughters in his naughty lap,
taking up the role their grandparents
grow too slow for. I can take them to that house
no longer.

"It doesn't cure itself," Sara says,
and Pam agrees. They both work
with victims and diddlers. "It's learned
and passed on through generations."
Something goes wild in the genes
through teaching. Then there is
the denial.
It survives through denial.
How can a child see past

the canopy of the family tree?

Before this year (one more rape
and the friendship of these women)
never reading the research, never trusting
my conclusions, I kept fumbling my flight
from this dysfunction of family;
never quite able. Yet
my lovers' names ink my skin
with a tattoo of feathers, dressing me,
inch by inch, in the apparatus of flight.
I am no longer covered in downy fluff
(so unsightly). In fact, my course
covers miles on the long,
slow flight
from that mussy
nest.

Bone Shards

for Al Purdy

Born near the last day of 1918, I imagine you
learning self-importance as a child or man.
You could always find a party for your birthday.
You learned to charm, to scalawag, to collect things
from the shelves in stores, later collecting
the hearts of women you wanted to explore
from the inside out.

What was it that turned you? Your mother did her
best, supporting you with income from the list
of homes she bought and rented, struggling
after your father passed, struggling more when you
brought home a new wife and child after breaking
with the one who delivered your first-born

Children scared you, your first so like your mad-hatter
uncle, the other, my brother, in a family of foibles.
So you orchestrated tricks, hiding tins your mother
wanted from the pantry, taking her money to buy
another. Your mother paid for your beer. You drowned
social unease in her denial of your scheming ways.

I imagine you walking in the woods close to home
as a youngster, learning to revere the trees, unable to
trust anyone else from birth until your passing.
On August 1, 1943, you were 25 when an Albino Robin
was found in Wellington, Prince Edward County,
the same Ontario backwoods where you were raised.
I imagine you the one who found it, raising it

from fallen leaves, turning it in your hand.

No cause for its demise determined, it was beautiful,
the feathers white as an angel's wing. No life to
persuade you otherwise, perhaps you were the one
who gave it to the museum — ROM 68599.
Then you passed on, not looking back.

You were 30 when my brother was born. He arrived
like a shard off the old bone, white and delicate
in my mother's arms. Ten months later,
you left them both, returning to an earlier tryst.
History says you never looked back. Yet that
was never true, that portrait of you as callous.

Mother told me of the letter you wrote to apologize.
She tucked it away with a photograph and the
document that declares your wedding day.
In 48 years of living with my father, a man she
truly loved, she never divorced you,
or you her — old bone.

Voice of the Land

in memory of Al Purdy

At times, I still hear your voice:
that low rumbling and distinct Ontario rhythm
rolls over hills and fields between the villages
of Prince Edward County,
like your shadow preceded by a clap of thunder.
In childhood, I heard of your Indigenous heritage
like so many Canadians. In that county
of farms and woodlots you lived close to awareness
of your Chippewa ancestors, a people who believe
language is born in response
to the land of one's birth.

How to reconcile your delight in language
— poem after poem, your special brand of candor —
with your innate knowledge of the land?
In '65, you were delivered to Canada like a prodigal son
returned from ice and snow in the land of the caribou.
In middle age, you built a summer shack
some call *the house Canadian poetry built*.
Years since your passing, crowds gather to celebrate
your verse and that hand-hewn home
with a picnic and endless eulogies.

My first memory of you — was a dead man
resurrected, newspapers delivering
a hero of Canadian conscience,
a frontier explorer, and award-winning poet.
Your news refuted all stories mother told
of a dead soldier, your absence explained

after you fled to Vancouver with her friend
and another family in '49.
In our family, we knew a man
the literati did not care to acknowledge.

Your son found himself a writer
before your shadow arrived with the paper.
In our family, tales were told
of a man who was difficult to love.
My brother wrote verses before he knew
his father still existed.
You were a mountain of a man,
the marriage forged with our mother
— never divorced —
rendered the rest of his siblings bastards.

He struggled with that distinct lack of recognition,
never able to escape the reach of your fame
even after your death.
Your marriage certificate
is buried in mother's cedar chest
like a fossil between strata.
We were raised to understand
our place in a legacy
that cannot be unmade.
I imagine your tombstone might say:

*Here lies a man returned to the clay
of his ancestors, forever restless,
dreaming of forgiveness.*

Prophesy

for my brother's father

Aged twelve
I dreamed of you
— my older brother's father —
a man who made his living
from words and innuendo.
I dreamed he and I were at a mall
making arrangements to meet
back at the central pool.
In this dream, that pool held a tree,
its bark stripped, branches naked.
And when we met again,
you stopped by with another child
— close to my brother's age —
explaining nothing to either one
though both were your sons.
Your greeting was light-hearted,
off-the-cuff, and soon we longed
to be away from this situation
of myth and denial.

We actually met years later,
and you were just like that dream
— sweeping in with bravado —
never thinking of consequences,
tearing other's lives apart.
You've passed over now,
reports on your method of leaving
straining those you've left behind.
So just now, I understand the dream

I had when I was twelve
as a prophesy
— the tree in the pool naked
no branches sprouting leaves —
and your sons had no children
so your branch of the family
has left the gene pool.

Maison des Fauves

in memory of
William McClure Brown, painter

When your sister spoke of your death
my first reaction was puzzlement, then tears.
You were still young. Just 54, you'd fallen
behind the curtain that so enthralled you
through life, that peek-a-boo covering
for the passage between this world and the next.
That drapery fell more solidly than it ever did
during our partnership in painting, as model
and artist — or model, artist and ghosts.
No longer gauze, it was suddenly impenetrable,
transformed into a gessoed canvas for your work
on the other side. I realized as she spoke
your death dug up a younger man,
for I had buried you deep in the decades
that slipped between us, you moving an ocean away.

Your daughter, in her 30s, had never met you
and never would, though you tried to find us
at least once or twice, discovering my parents
had moved, discovering your friend would lie
to protect us from your foibles, saying
he didn't know where we were.
Kathleen revealed you passed in July. That
is when I realized my unconscious hope
one day your silhouette would appear in my door.
I'd never given up the ghost of a dream we two
built as teenagers, now *disappeared*. Her news
was a tiny hole in a dyke designed to safeguard

against floods, a barrier to hold back the ocean
from land claimed beneath the waters,
a droplet built into weeping, a rivulet that suddenly
hemorrhaged in my tears.
I had preserved my love for you as a 20-year-old,
though I no longer knew who you became.

What I regret most are the elements you didn't
carry forward in your canvases, the decision made
to divorce yourself from what might have been us.
I imagine you watching canvases we made together
burn in a heap, discarded as trash, a relationship
deemed unsalvageable. I can only see your work
as cartoons, so much less than your early promise.
A friend suggests your work looks like the canvasses
of people who suffered a brain injury, and I cannot
swear it isn't true, for my own thought was
you suffered a type of lobotomy, loosing
your sense of purpose.

You devoted your life to canvas and woodcuts,
to the ink of your lino-prints and illustrations.
We-two had planned a journey in our teens,
though you left me and your children behind.
We built a *menage des fauves*, a house of beasts
that could not be tamed. You the philosopher
with a paint brush, commentator on everything
that struck you hard in life. You recognized power
in all that remains unsaid but hinted,
you rooted through legends and fairy tales
for the subjects of your work, after scaring yourself
with the strength of your own convictions
reading newspaper reports of war in the Middle East
or Vietnam. You, barely old enough to grow a beard,

were surrounded by those who dodged the draft
below our nation's border. We scared ourselves silly
reading Sartre and de Beauvoir, discussing
Berger's perceptions and the close realities
of *the artist as a young man*. We tasted the poverty
of making art in a power nation moving through
the 20th Century while struggling
to believe in itself.

I do not know the man you grew into being,
but I grieve the one who helped me define my own
dreams of what we can be achieved through art.
That is the you I miss, not the man who passed.
Night after night, I woke myself, grieving. Once,
my partner watched me crying in my sleep.
He could not believe I loved him more than
the dead man I cried for, failed to understand
it wasn't you I mourned, but the dream
we two had built together that I grieved.
The end of our potential caused my weeping,
for love and grief are inextricably linked.
As it turns out, I had more love for the art
than passion for the man, though
I never properly grieved my loss of either.

You left, and almost immediately I was a mother.
You were gone, but keep emerging
through your daughter, reminding me of our dream,
reminding me that the beasts we paint
or carve out of words hold the promise
of making anything that's gone
terribly wrong in this world
right.

April is Poetry Month

for AP

How appropriate to discover you died in April, the month
Canada celebrates the voice of poets. How fitting
to learn you're celebrated with a BBQ picnic
and eulogies, at that hand-built A-frame.

How opportune your shack is remembered as the house
Canadian poetry built on the shores of Roblin Lake
in a county made famous by cedar rail fences, dairy
herds, and thick-skinned wheels of aged cheese.

My first memory of you is a shadow creeping across
my brother's future, He read in the news of a man he
thought dead, delivered evidence to refute reason for
your lost connection, avoiding the son you fathered.

Married to my mother in Belleville, your home town,
abandoned for Vancouver and another family in 1950.
I grew up with stories others do not care to know,
my brother struggling to find himself beyond the edge

of your shadow on paper. Poetry called to him.
You were always a difficult mountain of a man, your
shadow cutting across his poetry, the rest of mother's
children rendered bastard offspring by your marriage.

Your marriage certificate proved his right to
acknowledgment as your son denied
that document buried in the bottom of a cedar chest,
a legacy un-recovered.

2

Boundaries

Summer Fever

one night an ex- throws a stone
against my window
to wake me

leaves his car running
across the street,
because he's unsure

I am pulled from sleep
by the noise of cats
screaming in their heat

Cured of Him

on this new street
with a new circle of faces
he is unknown, an existence
un-guessed rather than erased

I have doctored myself
with this change of address
knowing he is left in the cold
his effect is averted

he is like a chronic disease
returning, reoccurring
until the physician prescribes
a move to warmer climes

Exorcism

Even now
on my way to the operating room
he clutches my hand
with pleading
with reassurances

And fool that I am
I'm too polite, say 'I'm sorry'
but I need him out of my blood
and this time
it will be done

Like a poem
being bled to paper, exorcised
he's been removed now
pulled from my veins
softly

Unfreezing

The snow
is confetti on my shoulders
as I come into the room.

You speak my name
like an incantation echoed
between us, hold me
framed in the doorway
as snow soaks my collar.

You whisper my name
and it stills me with snowflakes
like rice in my hair
melting,
as your eyes unfreeze me.

Tectonic Invocation

a poem for two voices

who could deny the existence of angels
                guiding us toward our dreams
celestial bodies align in this cosmic conference
                as we come out of our long sleep
the earth itself moving
                shoulder to shoulder
whole planets shifting on their axis
                you rise and turn toward me
on this blue planet
                shoulder pressed against my breastplate
the shifting from night to dawn
                fingertips trace my hills and valleys
the whole of existence is audience
                as your shoulder shifts toward my hip
the friction of separate realities coming together
                all of our dreams manifesting
upon the physical plane
                the mid-west shivers, record snowfall
our lives the conductors of universal energies
                City of Angels sighs, its last hour of sleep
the friction of the earth's restless turning
                shudders run our bodies, you slide into me
rock plate slipping along rock plate at the epicenter
                all of our fictions come undone
in the moment of our two worlds colliding
                in our purpose and meaning
the planet rises real and powerful from a century sleep
                we are shaken from our dreamscapes
our lives manifest as metaphors of birth and destruction

extended in prayer or longing
and who could fail to see
even in the midst of great human tragedy
our prayers will be answered
when we surrender before the mystery

Rapture

mid-September
a night breeze stirs the curtain
every touch on our skins
rekindling
the chatter within
— muscles, hormones, memory —
our bodies still shivering
with the tongues of love-making
we lay magic and dumb
our faces beaded
and magnificent
the coal of your cigarette
like a torch to something
each of us had lost
and rediscovered

Spellbound

the heart whispers lyrical
        ventricles pounding
                flesh surrounding
        a dangerous phrasing
that admits us vulnerable
        the mind leaping
                in acrobatic musing
        I rise as blue dawn
cracks the black opaline
        sky still swinging
                on the pendulum
        of our passions
anticipatory
        struck by irony
                rising from your arms
        I am greeted by birdsong

When All the Clocks Stop

It is like a clock talking
        tock-tock, tock-tick
as we unwind on your bed

It is like a rich coverlet
we pull over our heads
        tuck-tuck in silken smooth,
        tock-tock, tock-tick
as we unwind on your bed

It is a wealth that stays
in your pocket when you're poor,
the way night drapes us
        in riches, in riches,
        tuck-tuck in silken smooth,
        tock-tock, tock-tick
as we unwind on your bed

It would be so easy
in the deepening of night
or the brightening of day
        if all clocks stopped
        tock-tock, tock-tick
        in riches, in riches,
        tuck-tuck in silken smooth,
        tock-tock, tock-tick
as we unwind on your bed

You want it to be now
when you're all unwound
        from tuck-tucking

In A Mist

it is the day after
and I phone
wanting to say
a new song
has nudged into place
though my children
play off-key tunes
in the other half
of my house
I phone
with all my senses
jazzed
by the gift of touch
that foggy cornet
a symphony
by Bix Beiderbecke
your hands
your mouth
surprises on my
waking skin
your face
your face in my hands
before we kiss
those notes
echo in my room
to lay down
blue jazz
on the day-long bed
instead
I tell you of
plants I bought
to fill the windows

the energy
in their green life
like Stravinsky's
Rites of Spring
informed by Beiderbecke
a Dixieland harmonic
and foggy cornet

Still Missing

for Robert Billings

Still missing —
I cannot think of that note
dated All Hallow's Eve
in any other context
I can't fight it any longer
short for saying
he was disappointed in
the life he walks away from
a man of routines claiming
Sometimes I feel
if I changed my pattern
like the invisible man
I'd be unseen

Still missing —
a man's bruised heart
walked him out the front door
I'm leaving now
another way of announcing
no one was listening
at critical moments
I scour his neighborhood
for two and a half weeks
posting bulletins
finding witnesses
the Police don't bother
to uncover

Still missing —
he had coffee
in a donut shop
a week after disappearing
three flirtatious women
unable to interest him
his next door neighbour
wondering why he stood
on the sidewalk watching
the street for hours
patient and expectant
— no one had been alerted
the man was missing

Still missing —
he seemed to search
for reasons to remain
hoping someone would find him
waiting by his own front door
the Police resisting our pleas, saying,
He's playing Silly Bugger
more than a week after
he mailed his note
— and how could he know
that desperate communication
would be ignored because
suicide is not a crime?

Still missing —
I'm going out where I came in the clue
he hoped someone could translate
friends and lovers sending letters
the phone still ringing
in an empty chamber

pleas printed in newspapers
from Toronto to Kingston
and his hometown Niagara Falls
Robert, we miss you, please call
coast to coast Canadian poets
striking up a collection
to hire a P.D.

Still missing —
in Toronto friends search bars
and hostels through late November
250 miles from home he's seen
on the shores of Lake Simcoe
honeymoon lake his heart was heavy with
as he attempted to unravel
the mystery of his adoption
on a small reserve
two weeks delayed the detective
shadows a man gone over
just to tell him
you're missed, you're loved

Still missing —
the money runs out
the P.D. confirming his attempts
to rework life patterns
his shadow crossing Ontario's map
the man gone invisible as if to start over
a final call alerting us all
to his reluctant decision
his obituary printed in late spring
when Niagara's whirlpool claims him
six months after leaving
— still missed

Such Sweet Sorrow

for RB

You were last seen the night before All Hallows Eve.
My father departed on Christmas morning.
Robert, you're one of two men who forever changed
my response to these seasonal celebrations
of birth and death, lending them new meaning.

We'd been apart a year, healing, moving on
when you came to my poetry reading.
I sang two lyrics to the pain of childhood.
You understood, coming home with me that evening.
We made love in a way that erased the malaise.

In the morning on the way to the subway you
wondered aloud if we could revive the way we once
loved one another. What did I say?
We parted, but I called you back, saying *It felt good to
reconnect.* You retorted, *Hindsight is 20/20.*

I watched you descend the stairs to another train
knowing I'd said the wrong thing
in a moment you had opened your heart.
Two days later, I learned of your letter
saying, *I am going out where I came in.*

I refused to believe you would leave that way,
remembering you once said, *I live by such habits.*
If I just changed my routine I would disappear.
I trusted you put that thought into practice.
I went out, day after day, to search for signs.

The detective hired to track you, caught up to your trail.
Just 1 ½ days behind you when the money ran out.
It was two months later that you hit the news.
Canadian poet presumed to have ended his life.
They found you in the whirlpool below Niagara Falls.

The coroner said you'd been in the water a few weeks.
You tried to flip your path, visiting old places
you loved as a different man. It didn't work.
You kept your promise, going out where you came in,
departing the city of your birth.

Dust to Dust

If we are made from dust

I would like to think
we are the dust of grain,
crushed by the weight of earth
in the up-turned bowl of the sky

And if we return to dust

I would like to be sowed in fields
like grain on the hard red clay
Perhaps I will stand as tall as corn
in a sun-ripening field

before returning to the bowl

Absolutions

Sylvia, I started from
an opposite end,
first the boy
then the forceps and pan.
This girl was my red carnation,
my long-awaited promise.
We both had that middle ache,
but my gas stove does not threaten
and it's wide enough to put
three heads in.

I can only imagine the cold linoleum
under your hip, the thick,
gas pillow with its stinging
swarm in your lungs.
The hypnotic gas-hiss
was your undoing,
you could not hear the babies
stirring in their upstairs room.
Their unfailing call — *Scheherazade* —
always brought you running.

Yes, you had your Frieda and Nick.
I had my far, bonny boy
and my promise —
though those blue robins
slipped from our nests.
I see the coincidence
but cannot wind my caramel hair
as sternly as yours.
Even for myself I find forgiveness.

Faith

wrapped in each other's arms
we stretch for words
that allow us to make
something beautiful or healing
out of this
our fear of consequences
stuffing the mouth
my single pillow shared by two
both of us knowing what goes on
in the heavy dome of my daughter's
head laid on my breast
ear to the dangerous whisper
of my heart when every man enters
or leaves this house like
someone come new to a city
with an address and a key
that somehow fits
but just inside he pauses
and neither of us
is sure this is that story
you and I with our kisses
like the key to a ready door
so we give each other the irony
of everything gone before this
the births and deaths
even the operations we hoped
would change providence
knowing the real key lies
in those children who wait
behind the wall of some fourth

dimension with balloons
candles on cake
and a wish
that only comes true
when you blow them all out
you and I decorate this bed with
the white filigree of our bodies
placing each candle
with the accuracy of love
that one for your son
those two for my daughters
these of a different colour
for the children we could not carry
this far into our lives
we name each one
with their real names because
every candle is more important
than its head of flame
and we are standing outside
a heavy ornate door
two people of no denomination
knowing inside this place
nothing is more important
than what is believed
knowing as we enter
there is still the question
of whether we belong here
we walk forward
to light our candles
and kneel
in simple prayer

Doubt

I am mapping the unlit areas within,
internal shadows, the incandescence
of opportunity and accomplishment
absent when self-doubt
inks the veins
drawing them dark as country roads.
I search for my own pulse,
finger on the nerve by my ear
finding its whisper — electric, magnetic —
in a current that wavers
primal and discordant.
Doubt is the song of a wolf
chained under a promising moon.
Doubt is old as humanity
but related to dogs
by unreasoning emotion.
It learned its black art
running at our heels
with the howl of impatience,
raising hackles
but failing in courage.
It is our insistence on easy endings
and simple plot lines.
Doubt is the hole in the cheese.
It is asking to be lulled
in a canoe on romantic currents.
So I speak to the perpetuation
of myths and our need
to unmake that teasing 'lover's moon'.
Doubt has its black moments
determined in its dementia,

unscrewing the stars
like light bulbs in an indigo sky.
Yet, its lunacy does not hold the moon
which is woman's calendar,
steadfast counselor and guide.
Moon cycle is the gift
some man named woman's curse
though we know it as our caretaker
in a meditative retreat.
Moon sets the waves to
constant turning, washing,
revealing and submerging.
In moonlight, our incantations
are cast like lace or a fisher's net.
Doubt is not the moon's disciple.
Doubt is a dog that sleeps in the sun
and calls for illumination
as night arrives with its magic.

Drawing Our Maps

> *what's a man to do with his own insides?*
> *How can he reconcile*
> *the girl and this moon,*
> *how can he put a world together?*
> *Roo Borson*

You are out there
under the reeling sky with its ritz,
one more man gone off on his chase.
    Dogs of exhaustion fur my mind,
    fatigue and isolation
    the arsenic in my tea,
    bitter without company.
        Shut-up with my babies
        any apartment is a box I am safely left in
        while you trip out.
            I talk to empty spaces, that one
            for instance
            a canine profile with ears like
        pyramids.
        Persistent hound
        he tracks my woman's curse like spoor,
        spraying musk on these sheets I tunnel in.
    As I peer out, his tongue rolls,
    a laughing growl,
    a kiss with barred teeth.
Why does he haunt me so?
He leads the pack
of shadows that thatch my room.
    Turned at bay and desperate —
    I will not get up.
    I will not get up.

> The dogs of insecurity
> have smelt my turmoil.
>> Sensing another man gone out
>> under the opalescent lure
>> of everything too distant to hold
> my cubs, little vixen, nudge and nip
> my teats in this dank den —
rabbit hole that Alice fell in,
tumbling past furniture of a kitchen
a woman asks herself questions.
What does a man want of me?
What does a man want of this?
> The baby suddenly hot
> and feverish, curds of vomit
> circling her head.
>> I rise to change her crib.
>> Tending to the ill one, I wash
>> her fevered face and sticky curls,
>>> her body so hot
>>> she resists my embrace.
>> How I long to hold your cool limbs.
>> Let me hold someone healthy
>> and be held. That's enough.
> But my nights are marred since the reading
> of poems you did not hear,
> your own art eclipsing
> everything else,
> my eyes on the door all evening.
Handshakes of strangers,
the words of strangers
do nothing for me —
> Thirty years in the incestuous shoe box,
> there is nothing they can do now
> but listen for the caught breath

of other children.
        Even now, you are out there
        with the whole world underfoot.
            Your head is tipped back
            to catch the whole night sky,
            those diamonds on black silk
            you hope to reel in.
        The head of this shadow nods.
        We both understand the distance
        breeding your perspective.
      You've locked yourself into orbit
      leaving me to tend to hearth and home alone.
The baby's voice runs my spine
like a volt, curds of vomit
surround her again.
        Shut-in, desperate, I strive
        for balance between lunacy
        and inspiration.
            I rise and fall back,
            rise and fall, like the oceans
            dragged up by the moon.

3

Oracle

Skin Deep/Batik

Her skin is white
as blank paper, or raw cotton
where she hasn't been touched

She wears the prints of fingers
and palms, hand prints of the men
who have lain with her

each one distinguished
by the colour of the bruise
though some overlap another

She looks like a life-sized
batik-print in seven different
colours, wearing those men

like a dress, skin tight

Cottoning On

I am *cottoning on* now
Your words gather in my ear
          like a soft white plug
Your mouth shapes sounds
          that do not tap in this ear
If I screamed at your back, leaving
          you would not turn
You've cottoned-on
You're looking for a lady weevil
          to eat my words from your ear

Quarter Moon

Night rings spirits in my ears
Metallic insects sing chring-chring
Voices rustle the dark like paper
Some call patiently, some are shrill
The house anticipates as I lie awake
And waiting, as if a guest were due
But they have all come and gone
Leaving gifts and birthday wishes
I am alone with this ringing in my ears
The throb of an abscessed molar
I am older, I am older
The shadows continue to rustle
Thin watercolour silks who call me
Chring-chring, moth by my ear
A coal in my mouth, pill on my tongue
Night stirs and whispers
Voices rub like insect wings
I can hear my heart, a long way off
Ringing like a bright red bell

Developing Life

Chosen for my skill, barely 20,
encouraged to dip multiple photographs
in liquids — bare-handed —
chemicals warmed to quicken the process.
I breathe those vapors for months
before realizing I am a vessel
for developing life.
My partner proud,
the news shared before
I notice problems:
back ache, daily spotting, cramping,
every breath like sandpaper in my lungs
— the effect of chemical toxicity
through percutaneous absorption —
my lungs and skin provide the wick.

Placenta privaevia, my doctor names
my condition, the magical link
— mother to child — blocking the cervix,
impeding the baby's passage.
From 12 weeks onward a fresh complication
— *placental abruption* — the link
between mother and child
tearing, I leak blood
with every exertion.
Two weeks in minor labour,
weakened, I cannot manage it.

My pro-life doctor, prescribes bed-rest
for 28 weeks. *I'll lose my job,*

my home. He fails to listen.
Something is wrong with this child.
If you don't help, I'll unbend a coat hanger.
That gets his attention.
He makes an appointment with his teacher.
That same afternoon, a renowned physician
grows angry finding no heartbeat.
He apologizes for his student,
sends me directly to hospital.
Something is wrong with this child.

I've talked of Robin falling early
as a featherless, half-formed bird.
The truth is, I didn't deliver him easily.
Tubes fed drugs to strengthen
weak contractions, chemicals
circulating a warm march
toward the resistance within.
Panicked for minutes, not breathing,
paralysis rose in my body.
It was fear, I might have hemorrhaged
without the intervention my first doctor resisted
or grown septic carrying a child
that passed, undetected.

Henry Morgentaler was jailed
a year later, his clinic bombed,
simply for providing options.
Over and over, I dream
of my unborn Robin
who opens blue eyes.

Two Songs, Almost a Lullaby

1

I dream our introduction while your ear
is still forming, the whoop-a-whoosh of my
blood pushing to enter your veins is the
first sound you will hear, your heart whispering
a rough imitation of mine until
your rhythm is established; embryo-wish
the machinery of my being groans
in recognition of your being there
the inconvenience of your parking
head to pelvis; you somersault! my hand
finds a form, you stretch your odd bubble
this space shuttle under my skin by which
you travel toward a small blue planet
with your arrival I can only say
welcome to earth, young spirit-traveler

2

child within, neither you nor I chose this
strange blue miracles weave my breast linking
us, the rush of blood through umbilicus
your skeleton and quick-fire of nerves, your
small heart beating since the 5th week; exist!
nothing less will do, child born through union
of man and woman protected in a
haven formed apart from tears, even in
the absence that marks your father's fears your
feet push against my ribs, to decry that
woman is made from man (that Bible lie)
whatever your sex it is my bruised ribs
the cage of my heart that insists you live!

The Bun in the Oven

for Brynna Kirsten Rene Berg

Dumpy icing bag,
they wheeled me to the elevator.

Five storeys up, God's steamy bakery waited,
closer to sky, where he could get his hands in.

I was bound for making a birthday.
Pat-a-cake, pat-a-cake, the baker's ready, mam.

I was not so sure. The whole floor hummed
with starchy coats. In the halls they were running.

Oh, the busy rush! The kneading, flesh of my flesh!
Bun-maker, bun-maker, send me a sweet roll.

Every hour they slapped bottoms gladly,
like my mother slapping doughy loaves.

Over-sized, I felt that huge hand squeeze my middle.
Twelve bells. We waited. The whole shebang waited.

Then one! two! three! she wafted in, made for eating,
pink and lovely as blind kittens mewling.

Ah, my sweet rosebud, we iced cakes then.
Yes, between us, we made a birthday!

Breastfeeding at the Art Gallery of Ontario

Alex Colville Retrospective,
Art Gallery of Ontario, Toronto, 1983

Even Colville could stand behind these gapers,
an intense study disguising the stippled face
looking out from the poster painting
fully armed.

I have brought my small family and Liz, a friend
who confesses she never considered art
before Warhol and does not think she will like this.
We stand before the first two, Liz reading
a biography posted before a circle of moving lips,
the painter's credentials in two-inch type.
Some speak under their breath, members of the gallery
plugged in to a recorded spiel, pass on,
every few minutes, as directed.

In one, a soldier lies in a quiet field, the slow step of
cows coming to him through frozen ground,
even they turn away now he is still.
In another, infantry slough through boot-sucking
marshes near Nijmegen. Someone behind me says,
I hate war. Her husband follows a tugged sleeve.

Liz catches my eye, her brow puckered
with unspoken suspicion. I shift the baby, Snuggli
holding her close to ribs instead of pelvis,
all the old aches still there.
Liz gives the soldiers another glance: reassured

they won't step off the canvas, the first in line
cut off at the knee, the weight of packs, greatcoats,
and sucking marsh slow their march.

My older daughter stands before scenes of nuclear
family — children and dog, husband and wife
back to back on the morning bed —
My baby fusses, rooting for breasts.
She cares nothing for convention or milling crowds.
Art students and senior citizens crowd the benches.
I consider leaving, then across the room,
a bench comes empty.

Liz and Ila follow the crowd, one painting to the next.
The baby mews and struggles. I think of Da Vinci's
controversial *Litta Madonna* giving Christ
a full breast, as people stand back
from Colville's *Refrigerator,* embarrassed
by a naked middle-aged couple
hunting for snacks after lovemaking,
cats rubbing ankles, silhouettes in refrigerator light.

Sitting before three sheep, long baas almost audible,
I slip Brynna from her Snuggli, positioning her to nurse
under the yellow-eyed gaze of the barnyard.
She finds my nipple, T-shirt bunched above her cheek.
I rock slow and easy, comfort sounds deep in her throat.
The crowd mills before Colville's work,
passing one year to the next.

An old woman stands by *Family and Rainstorm*
— a mother bundling her children into the car
as black clouds gather over steely cliffs across the bay.
She catches my eye across the room. I shy from

her frown. Behind my shoulder, a figure appears against
the light. Without looking I know a man bends to peer
at the baby latched to my breast. I turn,
allow him nothing but my back.

Ila and Liz return. I ease the baby from one breast
to the other. The old woman turns again to frown.
My baby suckles, uncaring. Horses run an eerie rail
here, a one-eyed monster closes the distance
as heron and crow wheel over boggy meadows
on wings that whisper ominous things.
Three shepherds gather with their flock, close bodies
in the smoky dusk. Black-frocked priest and blacker dog
watch over the still, cold bay as a woman
raises her hand. All stop for the cows, heavy udders
like purses between thin legs.

The old woman approaches as I raise my daughter
to burp her, the curd of spitting up on my shoulder.
Her voice is loud. *How old is your baby,*
dear? Eleven weeks? She must be
the youngest one here. You keep it up. Don't stay
at home. Get out and live.
Years ease from her face now. I can see her
nursing her babies behind closed doors,
a woman's breast signifying sex, her children unable to
tolerate cow's milk or a rubber nipple,
she nursed each one to the cup.

One child overlapped the next until her bedroom
became a place she spent years in.
Now Liz stands by a naked woman looking over
her shoulder at a dress dummy, the dummy
in the foreground life-sized. She says,

Don't you find this guy a little creepy?
I mean, this one reminds me of some dream I had.
The artist looks out from his self-portrait,
the menace of a gun on the table, but I am more
intrigued by a figure in yellow mask
and blue parka, the glove from his trigger hand
clutched in his teeth as he aims
at something unseen, off to the left.

Making Strange

*an infant's shyness or anxiety around strangers,
often resulting in crying; a passing phase
in natural development*

You have come
to visit your daughter
the smell of your lover

caught in the triangular
peninsula between your legs
the smell of runaway fears

like incense smoking the room
our baby looking up to a tall dark
stranger reaching down

lifting her into a burly
hug that frightens the shit
who is this man who

teared eyes turning back to me
in horror and suspicion
her expression telling you

in no uncertain terms
she does not know you
tears in her eyes saying

what I cannot say

Later the baby sleeps
nothing in my arms
but the distance from

my rocker to your chair
words lacing the space between
the memory of our bodies together

understanding growing between us
how we care — and how we care
the baby smiling next morning you kiss

her head against your shoulder
standing with my arms around
you holding your daughter

loving how we are
making strange
family groupings

Mirrors

his brandy an amber jewel in my glass
I sit in an old leather armchair
the comfort of pillows on the daybed
refused, my lover stretches out
on the floor

my child plays between us
reminding me of her distant father
I say, *He uses her like a mirror*
to fix his image by
whenever he passes through town

The brandy swirls in my glass, warms
like friction, lubricating my words
He says he can't just try…
it has to be all or nothing

What does that mean?
What is he afraid of? lover asks,
handing the baby her teething ring.
She's beautiful, I never thought
I could like another man's child

I run my brandy to the rim of the glass
and let it do the talking
Were you ever afraid of this?

No, never, he blushes, *I often thought*
it would work for you and me, if I were
a different sort of man

And what does that mean?
the brandy demands
his answer remains
unspoken

Tantrum

For days a crack in the plaster
has been temptation for her fingers
the rough patch balding while
she sleeps with long white slivers

I am the storm that reprimands
a reasoning anger
in response, the child blusters
Go to sleep, I demand

but the dark is wrong
my child hysteric
shut in her room
all reason come undone

I lie beside her, she crawls up
like a newborn rooting for the breast
her tiny fist clenched, hitting out
her sobs ragged as an old man's breath

Asking for My Hand

My older brother is on the phone.
My two-year-old is in the bath.
I hear the liquid plop of her hands
making waves for a green boat.
He is reaching out,
a man afraid of drowning —
he called because he has heard my poems.
Notes of need chime in his voice —
he knows I recognize that tune.
We are talking about our family.
He says he doesn't remember
so many things
and still claims damage,
knowing the things he's done to women.

My baby is talking to an orange bucket.
She shovels water into the brim,
her song just beginning.
I hear the squeak
of her butt on porcelain.
I can't stay on, I say.
The baby's untended in her bath.
We know how quick they go
in just an inch.
But he feels the undertow and sings
Who taught you your tunes?
He wants the answer easy.
His voice over the phone asking for
my hand — I hear the baby
screech on porcelain, her boat *Titanic*,
waves building, hands plopping,

that song just beginning.

He hears her, says,
You'd better go, but his voice
is the reedy flute of a man untended.
He longs for family, for mother-love,
for space on the raft I've built log by log
out of necessity.
My answer is unexpected.
Make a decision to embrace life.
The scream of her butt on porcelain,
the water just an inch,
the green boat and orange bucket,
the shovel shoveling,
bathtub waves building —
The baby chirrs, musical notes
of a slippery piglet,
rolling breakers awash in the tub,
just an inch,
an inch —
but knowing how quick they go
I tell him, *I'd like to help*
but just now
I've got my hands full.

The Dream

for Roxanne and Tilly Olsen

This is what I wanted to tell you.
I went back to bed while the baby napped
and in dream I rose from my body
to find you in your kitchen.
Light streamed through the window
as you stood at your ironing board,
orange hair piled high,
you were humming some tune
I almost recognized.
Then your husband arrived
saying he told some un-wifed man
you'd be glad to take-in his shirts.
You didn't look up from ironing.
He kissed you, saying it was his union leader,
he had to offer, or some nonsense
that made sense only in the dream.
He didn't notice your pale skin
hugging close to bone,
your eyes two shadowed moons
as you pushed that iron
over collar after collar,
a tiny boat on a sea of laundry.
When I spoke, your eyes turned up
smiling. You saw me (though I was only dreaming).
I said, *How beautiful you look*
with your hair springing from its pins.
Knowledge of your illness was a stone in my heart,
the look I wore made you tip the iron on its heel,

coming around the ironing board
to fold me in your arms.
We stood that way,
each hugging a vision of our own last breaths.
Friend, it was beautiful in that moment
to know we were going to be together
when we finally rested
in the great beyond.
Then I woke to the baby crying,
announcing it was time
to be getting on with things.

Forty Winks

My daughters have entered my sleep
— murmur of tiny engines I monitor —
one buzzy-soft with her sleep whistle,
the other gyrating to the pulse
of music the babysitter left behind,
almost catching rhythms
of the adolescent sex machine too early.
I seek the deep sighs and posture of sleep
on these dark night sheets.

Mid-day, it is impossible.
One engine might stutter and fail
launching the baby into vast silence.
The other mixes games with her tea party
of dolls and teddies, dressed in scarves
and dancing to a heavy pulse,
she parrots lyrics of love and sex
beyond her understanding.

I cannot sleep, fade in and out
on my unshared double bed,
the baby's stirring breaking into dreams,
the beat below stirring my unconscious,
the sleeping and woken halves of myself
mixing oddly like my daughter's
strange tea party.
Close to exhaustion after tending
the baby throughout the night
somehow my dream-play joists reality.
The baby mews for milk while my limbs

are filled with the warmth of lusting,
my children cross over the lonely rails
guiding this night train of thought.

Trying to recapture the sleep forfeited
for innocent company of words
and eyes saying *maybe, not yet,*
the music rises through the floor
sets my hips twitching,
night train screaming hard on twisting track,
blue daydream with a night whistle
even my children seem to hear
as, downstairs,
one daughter breaks into song.

Oracle: Lucid Dreaming

lover, the body reaches past itself in dreaming
to project remembered phrases of our limbs

the body having its own memory of events
played out upon our skins. With these two mouths

we search for three words in a tangle of arching backs
and eight appendages. Oh, we are revealed

to the inward eye. It defines us as both witness
and subject for the dream event.

In afterglow, bells of laughter pass under our windows
as refrain to the heart's lyric verses.

I turn to notice snow swirling deep into shadows
on arching winds, the dance of fireflies swarming

to mate in mid-air. And our spirits, alerted to
the code of dreams through shamanic teachings,

know a twinned soul resides in the body, one
traveling outward in our dreaming. These specks

of light like fireflies gathered outside our room
have come to witness and celebrate rites
more ancient than human studies of the moon. Yes,
even those who have passed over rejoice

whenever we couple to initiate love, or new life

Metamorphosis

Like children, we have taken books to bed,
reciting favourite poems, each to the other.
Later, we discover more than any author
delivers to the page as we stretch,
sheaf to sheaf, our faces beaded
in the shivering of our tongues.

Your friend has joked that you, of all men,
should be used to becoming fodder
for my poems. Only we two know the irony
in how many slip beyond the page,
candles writing their haiku upon the walls.
Rampant, ignored, my poems are moles
in a labyrinth beneath the skin.

In this tiny attic room, under the sloping roof,
we listen for snow melt, one note dripping
constant on tin outside the window.
You and I drift into stillness in the cradle of arms.
Lover, we each live but a moment in our search,
flecks of dust driven by winds,
yet we are more than breath and dust.

How to describe our metamorphosis?
You and I become the poem, both cadence
and rhyme inform our lives
as we dare to reach beyond the page.
Placed in cosmic currents
we sing the body electric with verse,
a haiku transfigured by candles.

Sand and Sieve

I lay my book on its belly
and walk through the dark house
past the children's door
the sound of their breathing
like moths against the light
— dangerously frail —
no way can I stand outside their door
the carpet already under my feet

the baby curls against
the far wall, the dark blotch
of scab and bruise around her eye
evidence of abuse or accident
— I cannot swear which —
her sister angry and hurt
by one more man gone absent
she resents my part
in not keeping him
reasons never being
reason enough to her
thinks she punishes me
time after time the baby
wearing bruises

I bend to kiss that face
the black moth that spreads its wings
over her eye in the thick air
of this breathless sleeping room

she stirs under my touch
her sister responds across the room
their dreams entwined
and loving the one who harms as well
in her own pain
I kiss her salty ear
and damp curling swirls of hair
above her troubled brow

this room is filled
with everything I have made
best out of bad choices
the life that grows by accident
or divine intervention
though every father shivers
with news of their conception
no man knows these children
as I do, and what is lost?
when I rise sleep-starved
pages on my desk wanting revision
my children receiving only half
my attention, a cold breakfast
chores of the house undone

after each interruption I turn
back to my room and reading light
the ink of their dark room
coloured sand in my vial, forgetting
the reason I passed down the hall
my children and my art a stronger call
than hunger or thirst
or the awful hours of doubt
and isolation, when one more man
says we demand

the essential energies he saves
for other purposes, for the willful
bitch of his art

the bitter nag is not my voice
never denying the hard thing it is
to be a provider
when even love and companion
have gone absent
and what there is to be done
is subjugated by black moths
in that sleeping room

4

Odyssey

New Year's Day

Sky like an Esher etching,
flocks of birds turn on the axis of their flight,
like schools of fish flashing silver under clouds.

An azure sky reaches into the first day
of a new year, while holding on to dark yesterday
as crowds of party-goers plant paper hats on heads.

They are going home after a long night
on someone else's floor.

Poetry

after the reading
coming back through the rain
the whole thing seemed
white and delicate
as the petals of Shasta daisy
and delphinium you touched
in the vestibule of the church
a shout of laughter
in the midst of a building
under reconstruction
those perennials gathered among
the boughs of orange blossoms
your fingers carrying
their perfume back home
your hands on the other
end of the baby's carriage
lifting as we navigated
stairs of the subway
lifting as we got on the streetcar
the child in her carriage
swinging between us
her older sister carrying a
flowered book of child's verse
the pollen on your fingers
we talked later about
things we wanted to acknowledge
but circled instead
making you say *if we became lovers*
the perfume of those flowers
unmistakable in any case
though nothing is simple
the carriage swinging

between our arms
the baby drifting off to sleep
before I lay her in her crib
her sister dreaming of verse
that will say all of this
what we manage is inadequate
words never achieving
what we dream of
though we will use them
sitting stiffly in our chairs
not kissing goodbye
though my arms are two long aches
your hands not touching
creases of laughter around my mouth
unable to form phrases
that used to come easy
16 and blurting anything
coming into our heads with this white light
sowing the quick white blossoms
of annuals that will not last the season
but this other perfume is dense
in my room, unsleeping
the streets of the city
dissolve between us
the pollen still there on your fingers
when you have gone to the far side
of what is possible
this perfume
coming into our dreams
for years and seeming to say
everything it is important to know
while the rain kisses
all green things
in their sleep

Rainforest: Vancouver 1999

Today a summer rain
falls in sheets,
the voice of ground
welcoming sky.
Nothing prepared me
for the orchestra of weather
in this region,
earth attended by music
under clouds from the ocean,
patterns and tones of rain
dominated by woodwinds,
the sheet music of a rainforest.
The mountains never distant,
summer rain on the cheek like a kiss,
but these trees demand attention,
inclining shaggy heads
to inscribe a harmony
between the land
and human concerns.

Anthems for The Homeland

in memory of Oka, Quebec, 1990

the bus travels northeast through rolling hills
a thin ribbon of highway curling over low drumlins
or cutting through the center of steep knolls
raw pink granite flanks bring me to shudder
as they pass the windows, this cruel road
stretched between two homes
doubling back on my path
I have boarded a bus to flee the attention
of a man who echoed my father's desires
going home for the opening of an old lover's play

under a gun-metal sky with clouds gilded at the edge
nature's purse spills nickels and dimes
over dark forested hills while rain patterns
the windows from here to there
even trees and boulders beside this wet road
distorted like a sodden papier-mâché
with smudged borders each silhouette
threatening to invade its neighbour

my old lover meets the bus, his kiss on both cheeks
a gesture between comrades
over lunch I share news not relayed by media
of a Toronto caravan rallying for Kahnewake
5,000 strong at Oka, Quebec

denied access to shade trees in the park
the spot we had intended to meet
the Sûreté du Quebec force us to offload
in an open field on the hottest day of summer
we learn later they followed the bus
to its motel pit stop, holding our drivers
at gunpoint by the road, refusing to speak English
in a search lasting five hours
cocking their rifles when a driver gestured
he was thirsty, pointing
to pop machines across the road

back at the rally, more Sûreté hide in trees
dark shadows surrounding the sweltering field
tension rising within the crowd
a sound system broadcasting
promises from politicians and First Nations leaders
I heard Elijah Harper's voice,
impossible to see him over the milling crowd,
frustrated by heat and community politics,
traditional women held private ceremonies
behind the podium controlled by men
gave a basket to women arriving by secret paths
said, *These four medicines will nourish your families,*
the baskets their version of seven fishes
and seven loaves

Lunch with my ex-lover is on a patio
by the mirror of a lake ringed in mauve mists
over blue hills, my older socialist lover unable

to understand the organizers' anger
as activists for other causes distribute leaflets
for *unity against the rape and pillage of the system* —
the politics of rock and soil unobserved,
every deep northern lake home to Mudjekeewis,
the land itself defining both language and tradition,
each greeting drawing upon generations of residence
in the homelands to acknowledge the presence
of Waynaboozhoo who named all things

the cosmos expresses rhyme and purpose
that mortals cannot avoid, my old lover is Lear
raping his daughter in the theater —
even as her sister stands to the side, reciting definitions
of infibulation and clitorectomy — the play
intends to contrast Lear's story with the political
rape of peasants in South America
at the back of the theater women giggle
as Lear writhes on the floor with his daughter,
safe to disagree under cloak of darkness
I applaud their ability to distance without argument
or tears, though the actors say afterward they
cannot understand the insensitivity
of some women in the audience

I intend to hold my tongue but he asks,
this old lover, old enough to be my father
suddenly I understand what he knows of women
is discovered through their bodies,
unable to fathom their anger or humour —

in that dark theater part of me retreated, safety
in distance when no one is trusted,
he cannot understand appropriation, the artful
reflections of self in the script obliterate the other
this is the same thing that happens
on the road through every reserve
where the people have weathered centuries of denial
before erecting barricades

a bullet claims the life of a Sûreté officer in Quebec
it remains unowned, or disowned,
an accidental shooting bringing The Pines
(the graves of Mohawk ancestors) to center stage,
it makes Canadian history as the army arrives
to replace the Sûreté holding an entire village
hostage, a battalion sent into the woods to secure
a putters' green as soldier squares off with warrior,
unblinking First Nations remember the baby born
at Wounded Knee, protesters surrounded for 71 days
in 1973, in 1990 an ambulance is stopped on the bridge
at Oka and regular citizens force a Mohawk woman to
spread her legs to prove she is having a difficult birth

78 days of protest at Oka, Quebec, in 1990
disagreements untended since New France
awarded that land to a Sulpician Seminary in 1717
a land grant protested by Mohawk time and again,
no respect shown for the graveyard
beside a city-built golf course, the Mohawk
taking up arms only when expansion

threatened the bones of their ancestors

Oh, Canada! Vast stolen Native lands
Ours by decree of a foreign king's command
Their nationhood, England's crown denied
Though we postured with treaties
and the people were, oh, Canada
denied their own ancestry!
The crown holds the land, the Natives dependent
on Canada by denial of their sovereignty!
Oh, Canada, at Oka they resisted our army!

Sugar

it only makes sense
they took what they needed with them
— not the explorers who risked their lives
but those who settled the land —
took what they needed in comforts
and provisions, including the workforce

downtrodden Irish and British thieves
brought to serve their sentences in a useful way
often died, stuffed in the ship's hold
or simply unable to take tropical heat
on those foreign fields

so the rich began importing others
people who tolerated heat in their homelands
people who were bullied into the cane fields
often sold by neighbouring tribes as money,
power, and excess were the root of slavery

sugar started the trans-Atlantic routes
of ships, marking the map of slavery
for sugar cane that grew on hot and humid lands
but sweetened afternoon tea and treated
the highborn with fancy cakes and pastries

Jubilant

poem, based on an editorial by Dorothy Day

Mr. Truman was jubilant, President Truman
true man being our reference to Christ as true God
true man of his time in that he was jubilant
not son of God, brother of Christ,
certainly not brother of the Japanese
jubilanting as he did. He went from table
to table on the cruiser bringing him home from the
Big 3 Conference, telling of the great news.
Jubilant, the newspapers said,
we have killed 318,000 Japanese.
Jubilate Deo, we have created.

The effect is hoped for, not known,
hoped our Japanese brothers are vaporized
men, women and children scattered to the Four Winds
over the Seven Seas. Perhaps we will
breathe their dust, feel them on our faces
in the fog of New York, in rain on the hills of Easton.
Jubilate Deo, we have created.
Nature had nothing to do with it,
destruction born in the midst of tempest
and lightning on the desert.

We have created, not that man might live,
President Trueman announcing — jubilantly —
it cost two billion. The greatest scientific gamble
in history, and we won. A bomb dropped
on an island in the eastern hemisphere
on the Eve of the Feast of the Transfiguration

of our Lord. Jesus Christ, the newspapers
list the scientists, the atom smashing gun found
unnecessary in the end, not sledgehammer blows
but subtle taps from neutrons managed
in a tuning technique.

The atom of Uranium 235 smashed with surprising ease
reminiscent of stories that one violin note
could collapse buildings if found, reminding us
God's voice is heard not in earthquakes but
the whistling of gentle air.
Scientists, army officers, universities,
captains of industry, all are given credit. Great Britain
controlled Uranium ore from Canada and Rhodesia.
We made the bomb that would be used for good,
newspapers filled with descriptions of a new era
with pictures of industrial towns where parts
are made. In the foreground of Oak Ridge, Tennessee
a chapel benignly settled beside the plant, even
scientists in the desert kneeling to pray. Yes,
God is still in the picture.

God is not mocked on the day of this news. God
made a madman dance, breaking a silence of 20 years,
sent a typhoon to damage the carrier Hornet, a
bomber crashing into the Empire State Building in fog.
these things must also be remembered, our lives
in the hands of He who created as well
as we who have created.

Turning to the Vatican for judgment we forget
our Lord already pronounced when John and James
called fire from the Heavens upon their enemies,
You know not of what Spirit you are, the Son of Man

come not to destroy souls but to save.
And he said, *In as much as you do it unto others*
you have done it to me. Over and over
in history, this slaughter of the innocents.

Over and over, groups who believe Judgment
is upon us today, or next month, or six months
from now; in times of the Apostles, believing
Christ would return they prepared, Christians selling
their belongings to live in common. St. Paul cried,
Who will deliver me
from the body of this death? this life
looked upon as the womb, the life to come,
our release from bondage.

Glorious cities of the past have fallen,
Ur of Chaldees, Babylon, cities of the Egyptians,
Jerusalem the Golden. Down in Washington,
a Conference is beginning, the great ones of the Earth
confer, yet ordinary people wonder
when should we depart
like Lot escaping Sodom and Gomorrah?

Entregarse

*from the Spanish: abandon; surrender oneself;
yield to something*

We are equations of the sun.
Without touching, our hands play a global chakra
the resonance between us like harmonic chords
of a galactic guitar. Dreaming an astral music
we travel hills and valleys,
the rhythm of our bodies spontaneous
and sonorous as the water drum.
Breath, water and dust,
we braid a unity, generating tones unheard
even as they manifest.

Standing beside a polluted river we watch
the muskrat fish, reminding us of
Muskrat's ultimate sacrifice in the Midewiwin
legend of The Flood, for the sake of community
and Earth's Second Creation.

Later, in a small café, we talk of the power
to rebuild: self-supporting orphanages
in Mexico, co-operative farming in Africa
or India, sovereignty returned to the colonized
in Australia, the West Indies, the Americas.

Suddenly we emanate light,
its pink bubble surrounds us, drawing
smiles from the waitress, telling friends
there is hope for the world in the love between
two people, in the joining of our cultures.

We know that culture is humanity's love song
for the homelands, each song unowned,
made for giving and forgiving.
Listen, the Earth
resonates like a mother crooning.
She is calling home her prodigals.

In loving, the song of the universe fills us
to overflowing. We become the third sphere
and axis between the physical
and spiritual worlds. Love is both
our anchor and our progression, a pure light
launched on the bow of our bodies
to pry the narrow door to another soul.

We are both the intention and the witness,
the conscious participants in Creation's dance.
The body is a site of worship in all religions
of the physical world. Together, we generate
a resonant choir of praise and wonder. Together,
we emerge from darkness
in a glowing flame of love
for the world
and all its people.

I am saying *Yes,*
giving myself to what *Is* —
entregarse, the integer,
the *whole*
that is holy.

Odyssey:
Contemplations The Angels Have Not Left Us

for Hugh McCullum and Pauline Shirt

1

To my question, Rebecca replies
There is only the one story.
This is how we make sense of it.
Hundreds of bodies pour over the falls,
revealing the war upstream
as Hugh writes from Nairobi in the spring.
It is 1994. In this family
we ask questions of the one
who has been there, Rebecca's partner,
my daughter's grandfather,
an international journalist and Church worker.
His letter arrives in April, when even
this family still thinks of Rwanda as a country
made famous by gorillas in the mists
on forested mountains.

2

The world's maps are being redrawn
with the massacre of Tutsi civilians. in his letter
Hugh reveals he was on the relief plane
evacuating Canadians: aid workers, diplomats,
nuns and the orphans they refused to abandon.
There is only this story in the beginning,
the river revealing a slaughter
long before roadways became streams

of refugees seeking shelter
beyond a tiny, war-torn country.
The rest of the globe is watching television
as they collapse from exhaustion
on the lava rock at Goma, where cholera
claims them through the contamination of water.
And the truth is horrible,
for this is just a paragraph
in the story of a river.

3

For 28 months the blue helmets of UN soldiers
have bobbed between Serbs and Croats
in the ethnic wars of Bosnia, trying to
foster peace where scraps of land are claimed
through the rape of women and children.

Around the world, the liquid seed
of men contaminates the gene pools
with hatred while the rivers never cease to babble
that the health of rich Americans is reclaimed
through the disappearance of South American
orphans sacrificed for organ transplants.

The negotiations of Israel and Palestine
or China's occupation of Tibet,
or the civil uprising at Oka, Quebec,
or the struggle for a free vote in South Africa —
all are paragraphs
in the story of a great river
that over spilled its banks
to cover the Earth.

4

This is our odyssey: call it *River of Life*
or *Stream of Consciousness*. It is a strong current
that eddies and pools near the edges.
We arrive to this plane
with a destination and no boat.
We arrive with all conscious maps erased.
We have only the one task.
At birth, our shadow slips ahead of the body,
a forerunner, foretelling the future in dreams.
It is a twinned heartbeat that taps
the rhythm to pace this journey. If I say
I recognize you, it is because
our shadows have gone ahead,
shoulder to shoulder in the river.

5

Water finds its own level.
We forget the human body is 70% water.
We forget the Great Flood is upon the Earth
as we speak. We've neglected
the complexities of water, though
we persist in rerouting the planet's arteries.
Acres of land are desertified daily by lumber kings
but the mountains shave mansions from their thighs
in mudslides, the floodplains of the Mississippi
awash in floating cars and collapsed buildings
with every spring rain.
Thinking we will master water,
we have barely learned to swim.

6

We had forgotten the physical world is more
than a plane to act upon, more than illusion.
The Earth itself is our task.
Remember?
Call it our gift. Listen
to the river that chatters within,
your body a skin filled with water.
Water and wine are
the blood of the host.
We are one with the host.

7

My prayers rise on tobacco smoke.
Only in circular breathing does this pipe stay lit.
*Let the channels clear so I can be delivered
to the current. Place me as a stone
in the bridge between cultures.*
I heard it almost before I answered the phone.
No matter whose voice was on the line, I knew…
this was the river calling.
All across the planet, we rediscover water
though we struggle to find the language
to describe it.

8

Some call it love, others call it God,
a friend says, referring to the way
our paths have crossed.
Jung called it synchronicity, I respond,
knowing that all of this is the river.
We should not be surprised,

each drop finding its own level, even as waves
of humanity pour into the world's cities.
We know the Inuit have dozens
of expressions for snow,
which is only
crystals of water.

Some talk of guardian angels,
some talk of destiny.
Some dream they have a world-cruise ticket
that only stops in safe harbours.
We know the river has patience.
We know it doesn't take those who
stand on shore.
My shadow is already ahead of me.

Acknowledgments

I offer my sincere thanks to Mary Frost for her keen eye and editorial skills, which helped to finalize the text for this book. I also offer my thanks to Maureen Hynes for offering some suggestions and to Tom Gannon Hamilton and Stuart Ross for their editorial input on earlier manuscripts for this book. Plus,I am truly grateful that Tomas Lollike allowed me to use his wonderful photograph, which perfectly suits being the cover of this book.

Grants from the Ontario Arts Council received during work on this manuscript (recommended by Coach House Press, Wolsak & Wynn Publishers, Cross Canada Writers' Quarterly, and Fireweed in the 1980s) were instrumental to my ability to focus on the initial versions of many poems in this manuscript. I also acknowledge an old 'B' grant from The Canada Council and scholarship support from the Banff Center (also in the 1980s), which allowed me a period of residence at The Leighton Artists Colony to work on poems in this manuscript.

After a long hiatus from publishing poetry books, a grant from the Ontario Arts Council through Porcupine's Quill in 2019, assisted in creating the final manuscript for this book. This book has been in-process since 1984. Some of these poems had periodical publications, including: Big Pond Rumours E-Zine, Cross Canada Writers' Quarterly, Dandelion, Grain, Otherwise Engaged (Mexico), Poetry Canada Review, Roundyhouse (Wales), Setu Magazine (USA/India), and The New Quarterly.

Some poems were featured in audio recordings such as: Black Moths, Public Energies, Ottawa (1986). They were released again on the CD Sharon Berg: the re-published audio recordings, Big Pond Rumours Press (2006) and in its accompanying chapbook (2006). Other poems first appeared in anthologies such as: Concrete Mist 2019 Anthology, edited by Heath Brougher, Concrete Mist, USA (2019); Tamaracks: Canadian Poetry for the 21st Century, edited by James Deahl. Lummox Press, California, USA (2018); the GritLit Writing Contest Chapbook, Ontario, Canada (2016); Paper Reunion: An Anthology of Phoenix: A Poet's Workshop (1976 — 1986), edited by Sharon Berg & Julie McNeill, Big Pond Rumours Press, Ontario, Canada (2016); and Arrivals: Canadian Poetry in the Eighties, edited by Bruce Meyer, Greenfield Review Press, NY, USA (1986). Two chapbook publications included several poems in this collection. They are Black Moths (Big Pond Rumours Press (2006) and Odyssey and Other Poems (Big Pond Rumours Press (2017).

Four of the poems won 2nd Prize for Poetry in the 2017 GritLit Writing Contest, Hamilton, Ontario, Canada, and two poems received Honorable Mention in the Stellar Literary Festival for 2007 and 2008.

Finally, there are a few borrowed lines from other authors' work. The poem Drawing Our Maps has an epigraph from Roo Borson which is used with her permission. The title In A Mist is borrowed from the Jazz cornet player Bix Beiderbeck`s composition of the same name. In the poem Metamorphosis the last verse borrows from the title of Ray Bradbury's Science Fiction novel, I Sing the Body Electric. The final three lines of Stars in the Junkyard are borrowed from the song Nature Boy, made famous by Nat King Cole. The title Odyssey: Contemplations the Angels Have (Not) Left Us argues with the title from a book written by my youngest daughter's grandfather, Hugh McCullum. He wrote The Angels Have Left Us: The Rawanda Tragedy and the Churches (2004), World Council of Churches.

Sharon Berg is a poet, a fiction author, and an historian of First Nations education in Canada. She's published her poetry in periodicals across Canada, as well as in the USA, Mexico, the United Kingdom, the Netherlands, India, and Australia. Her first two books were poetry published by Borealis Press (To a Young Horse, 1979) and Coach House Press (The Body Labyrinth, 1984). This was followed by two audio cassette tapes from Gallery 101 (Tape 5, 1985) and Public Energies (Black Moths 1986). She also published three chapbooks with Big Pond Rumours Press in 2006, 2016 & 2017. Her fiction appeared in journals in Canada and the USA. Porcupine's Quill released her debut fiction collection 'Naming the Shadows' in the Fall of 2019. Her cross-genre history 'The Name Unspoken: Wandering Spirit Survival School' was published in 2019 by Big Pond Rumours Press and received a Bronze 2020 IPPY Award for Best Regional Nonfiction in Canada East. She lives in Sarnia, Ontario, Canada.